PRAISE FOR *AT DUSK*

Fran Claggett-Holland's *At Dusk* speaks directly to the vast landscape of the heart. This collection is an epic poem containing a clear-eyed chronicle of human experience. Hidden deep within, its lines are guides for inhabiting our bodies and celebrating the music of everyday life. Fran's poems are landscaped with spirits traveling both inner and outer worlds. Her poems weave together myth and dreams. Though Fran's poems are filled with remembrance and transcendence; she always knows her way home.

In his later years Stanley Kunitz wrote "I can scarcely wait till tomorrow when new life begins for me as it does each day, as it does each day." Fran also exudes this remarkable vitality and it is apparent in her poetry.

Fran's poetry is magic in words, a testament to her mastery and ability to touch the very essence of what it means to be alive and to celebrate it.

Les Bernstein
Poet, Anthologist, Editor

AT DUSK

At Dusk

Fran Claggett-Holland

San Francisco, California

© 2026 Fran Claggett-Holland

All rights reserved

ISBN 979-8-9921594-7-9

Part II: "To Paint the Shadow of Circumference" is a nod to Emily Dickinson's concepts of Circumference and the Absolute.

Part II: "Under the Shadows of the Night" was written in response to Edward Hopper's "Night Shadows" for Reverberations III at the Sebastopol Center for the Arts.

Part III "Woman Moving out of her own Mythology" was written in a workshop conducted by Robert Bly in which he distributed an uncooked vegetable to each participant to use as a stimulus for a metaphor in a poem.

"Beyond the Canvas" is an ekphrastic poem written in response to a work by the Ethiopian artist Tiemar Tegene.

"Given a Choice" is an ekphrastic poem written in response to Wilfredo Lam's "Bodies of Work."

The author wishes to thank Charlie Pendergast and Kevin Connor of RiskPress Foundation for their continuing support.

Cover artwork by Tamsin Spencer Smith

Author photo by Laurie Plant

San Francisco, California

Dedicated, as always, to Madge Holland;

Warren Bellows, whose art illumines my walls and whose questions illumine our philosophical lunches; and

Michael Franco and Freeman Ng, my two sons, who give me so much happiness in allowing me this role in their creative, productive lives.

You, the Poet
Dust off all things animate
Beautify with time earned
Life blesses the Poet

You, the inherent poet
create beauty
for all the times reimagined
in another lifetime

"Reverberations of Love" –Gishe Reyzl and Petra

CONTENTS

PART ONE

Breakfast in Venice	1
Observations from my Chair	2
The Cycle	3
The Green Gladiolus	4
The Canopy	5
Origin of Vowels	6
The Transmutability of Form	7
This Consciousness that is Aware	8
Crow Crossings	10
After the Storm	12
On the Card from Paris	13
Owning the World	14
Among the Multitude	15
Unsteady Beauty	16
Until the Magician	17
Introducing Felicity du Fleur	18
Felicity du Fleur, at a Poetry Reading	19
Felicity has Something to Say	21

PART TWO

To Paint the Shadow of Circumference	23
At Dusk	24
Shadowed Stars	25
Under the Shadows of the Night	26
The Story Goes Like This	28
On the Origin of Ritual	29
Ars Poetica I: Living on the Edge of Mystery	30
Ars Poetica II: On the Edge of Mystery	31
Generation	32
Afterthought	33
Digging to China	34

The Shadows of Love	35
To Live in Exile	37
Dream Data	38
Soundings	40
Wolf Speaks in Myth	41
Untranslated Language	43
The Predicament of Being Human	44

PART THREE

Fragility	47
Moving into Language	49
Woman Moving Out of Her Own Mythology	51
William Ernest Claggett	53
Adagio Cantabile	55
I Took Her Name	57
A Memory	58
On Turning 96, I Ask	60
To Ted Kooser	62
The Crooked Tree, Revisited	64
After Words	66
Not a Sonnet for Margaret Rooney	67
Beyond the Canvas	69
Ekphrastic Rendering	70
Like Neruda	71
Words, Once Written	72
The Same Image, Over and Over	73
When One Outlives the Other	74
On the Edge of Time	75
Field Guide to Memory	76
Saying the Unsaid	77
Madgik, My Saluki	78
Just Before Dying	81
Until	82
Clarity	83

PART ONE: FROM MY WINDOW

BREAKFAST IN VENICE

I woke up to a foggy day and to your words, along with the words of Marcus Aurelius, as read by Brunetti, the Venetian policeman who reads Aurelius before breakfast, and I am in the café with him and coffee and a brioche. I was soon aware that I was not reading Donna Leon for the story but for her magic way to transport me to Venice and to the awareness of her way with words. It is seven in the morning, and I am alone and I have coffee but no brioche. Still, I have Donna Leon and Brunetti and Marcus Aurelius, whom I know only through Brunetti. And for some unknown reason, I have you to share my small table in the café in Venice.

OBSERVATIONS FROM MY CHAIR

plum tree outside my window
bends in the storm
blossoms touch the ground

iris bud growing
suddenly thirteen
shades of purple

on the fence
stretching above
two red squirrels

there is no end
to the burgeoning
of three-legged haiku

visiting wren
just flew away
leaves still fluttering

THE CYCLE

When I wasn't looking
the tree outside my window
burst into flowers

once again
when I was not attentive
I see the cycle has begun

flower - the beauty
berry - the birds
seed - the promise

will I live to see beyond the flower
and hopefully the birds
to the promise, scattered on my deck

THE GREEN GLADIOLUS

Do you know the green gladiolus
how you think it is yellow until
under the passing sun
you see its essential self
that pale transparent firstborn
green

THE CANOPY
for Warren Bellows

here there is only today
edging into tomorrow
flaring into great slabs of sky

the canvas awash with wonder
blue green umber violet sienna
green so dark it becomes black

white swatches tumble past
the trees rooted in redolence
spreading out to create a canopy

intertwined
against the sun rising
and falling

white water stretches everywhere
creating great clumps of life
waiting to burst forth

ever more serious
ever more playful
never in repose

ON THE ORIGIN OF VOWELS
in 750 BC, the Greeks added vowels to the Phoenician alphabet and the combination was regarded as the initial true alphabet

    before vowels
    the names of things were
    held tight by consonants
    words heavy with dark
    sunken sound

on the edge of the horizon
sound dredged from deeper waters
brought new buoyant consonants
emergent, verging on the
unknown

    birds with rainbow plumes
    oceans of wings
    came with intricate song
    carrying waves of vowels
    completing possibility

THE TRANSMUTABILITY OF FORM
for Warren Bellows

How is it that I am looking at a painting
all muted blues with black and white
brush stroke splotches here and there
nothing reminding me of why I chose
this particular composition although
its movement captures my eye

but then, sitting in my usual chair
I looked up again and there in my blue
black and white abstract was the
head of an arctic moose
flinging ice-encrusted blackbirds
into the emerging spring

did the painting change?
did my eyes change?
are we all artists of our surroundings
of what we see
of what we have seen
what then of reality
of truth
what then of the artist flinging
paint off his brush into such
transmutable ineffable form

whoever even heard of an arctic moose?

THIS CONSCIOUSNESS THAT IS AWARE
for Robert Duncan

hearing his voice
again and again
as I heard it the first time
long before I knew him
long before I had any idea of the meaning

of the words   his high frenetic voice
stunned me with knowledge
so dark and deep and vast
I fell into the power and beauty
of primordial myth

I do not analyze the fabric of those
stirrings, hearing the unending rapture
of language, of poetry, of myth
encompassing everything I knew
and everything I did not yet know

always I am permitted to return
to his meadow and know it for the first time
know again the poem that became the falconress
conveying the ecstasy
of ultimate pain

waking now to the end of my beginning
I measure out my days

grounded in rhythm and rhyme
grounded in deep structure--
in this consciousness of form

CROW CROSSINGS

for Doris Cross, the artist of columns, and others who have crossed my life with crows

Framed, a column of
word, a column of
bird, scavenger of black
birdwords transforms,
blackens the dictionary page,
illuminating word and bird.

In the letter, a feather, black,
glossy with the sheen of the
Puget Sound crow; the poem,
feather-flown, crosses the
black track of words,
molts on the white page.

Eleven thousand three hundred
twenty-seven feet, crossing
the divide, two crows, tree-
top static, white in the
snow, suddenly scatter
inked wings.

The legendary Lake country:
Turn here, she says, to her husband,
her first time in this part of England
although he was born in Oxford.

Now here. Left, not right. Just ahead,
there will be a sacred circle of stones,
a small Stonehenge.

There was. And in the center,
                    the single, black feather.

AFTER THE STORM

I woke to a rainbow
and light drizzle, checked the horizon
the dawn redwoods with their surfacing roots,
the tall pines upright again after swaying
through the night, the wild plum,
the Chinese privet remaining steadfast
although sweeping almost to the ground

I knew the cedar waxwings had become dependent
on the small dark berries that litter my deck
after the storm, and I have become enthralled
by the sequence of robin and privet
throughout the yearly cycle
fragrant flowers, berries that brought
the migrating birds to the window where I now sit
in my chair, no hiking these days,
just watching the storm come and go
leaving that rainbow
stretched
across the sky.

ON THE CARD FROM PARIS

the woman
the guitar
the voice
she sang beyond the genius of the sea
      the poet wrote
you will love her, everyone does
      I heard
we have many friends
      you said
you sang to my deaf ear and I heard the song
      sweet and pure
as the multitude heard it when you sang to them
you, the child of eleven, even then singing beyond
      the genius of the sea
and still, you, the woman everyone loves,
      cannot stop singing
and I, when no longer in this dimension,
      will carry your voice, clear and true,
          and the voice of multitudes
      because I have become part of
          everyone

OWNING THE WORLD

Whatever room she was in
she claimed as her own
Hands full of daffodils
        pulled wildly in the joy
        of taking all color into her world
Owning the world
        owning the living which is equal
        to owning the morning sky
when all the stars have disappeared
        into the sun and dreams emerge
        from that formidable light
Draw light.
Draw living.
Draw death.
What color is the sun when it is sleeping,
What color the earth where she is walking.
What sound echoes in this hallowed place
giving voice to the living
        and color to the dead.

AMONG THE MULTITUDE

standing in the midst of thousands
waiting for the puff of white smoke
I ask. why am I here? I am not Catholic.
I am not Italian. I am a believer
but not of any doctrine.
So, why am I here, in St. Peter's square,
 surrounded by all these people.
and then I was transported back.
I was twelve, alone in an unfamiliar church
I heard the word bishop and looked up
Into his bluer than blue eyes
and he, dressed in white and crimson
unlike any preacher I had seen
and in his hands, a great gold cup studded with
colored gems. But instead of offering
the cup to me, he put it down and put his
huge hands on either side of my head
and held them there, then smiled and
nodded toward my seat in the pew.
And then I looked around me and I was
in St. Peter's square, along with the multitude
waiting for the puff of white smoke
and the man in white and crimson
with blue eyes

UNSTEADY BEAUTY

Vermeer mulled
two blues
one for the heron
the other for the sky
into which she flew

grief
like the great blue
awkward in rising
bound in this tight poem
unsteady beauty

do you know
how much I love you
she asked
do you remember the time
the time when

use both hands
grief in one
beauty in the other
place both on her heart
breathe

UNTIL THE MAGICIAN

what is love that does not bleed
that holds the space for touch
that holds its breath beyond the break

what of love that does not cry
that extends the silent moments
standing there

alone with the Fool
the dog at her side
above the abyss

INTRODUCING FELICITY DU FLEUR

Pulchritudinous. now there is a word for you.
too flowery? never. I wasn't named Felicity for nothing.
Just look at me. Flowers everywhere.
You have to wade through armfuls just to get to me.
Who says Amsterdam is too tulipy. People pay a lot
just to inhale the odor. But who really likes tulips?
They are too harsh. Felicity prefers lavenders. yes, with an s.
You thought lavender was singular, didn't you.
Wrong. Just look at Warren's painting "Lavender at dusk."
There must be a hundred variations of lavender in that
exploration of lavender just at the moment of utmost
variation. not a flower in sight. That's the way I like my
name, color, contained in all of its possibilities.
Water, air, tree, ocean, moon. See how it changes?
just like my name. Never the same twice.
As you shall see.

FELICITY DU FLEUR, AT A POETRY READING

just the other day, at a poetry reading
organized by our own Ed Coletti at the
Frida Cafe, yes, that Frida, we see her
always in pain in her art, married to
Diego, but he had nothing to do with
her pain, well, we don't know, do we.
but she gave her name to this cafe, made for
poetry, with a stage and shade, just perfect,
anyway, as I was saying, the other day,
Sunday, it was, the poetry lovers of Sonoma
were there to hear some of our wonderful
poets, well, Ed himself, read and I must tell
you, his poems were, well, simply said, the
absolute best we heard all afternoon, so good
I can't wait to read them in print, not only the
one about crows, since he and I both know that
is a winner, but the second one, and I can't recall
the title, but it was, well, just great, a totally fine
poem and I should know, because although my name
is Felicity du Fleur, it might as well have been
Felicity du Poetas because I know a great poem
when I hear it and I heard Ed read it last Sunday,
but what I really want to tell you today is that
every time I lifted my eyes to the wall, the WAll
at the entrance of the Cafe, the whole wall, the
entire bank of it was shimmering with a deep deep
beyond the pale purple flower, an absolute purple

totally covering the wall...on and on, as far as the
wall went, as far as Ed's poem took me,
Felicity du Fleur/Poetas at this, Frida's purple cafe.

FELICITY HAS SOMETHING TO SAY
after reading Ada Limón

reading your poems
I imagine living your life
it is real, your life - so unlike
mine I imagine my life as
unreal and yours the reality
all those cars, no, motorcycles
we thought only other people
revved their motors, raced down
residential streets where I lived
and eyebrows shot up and I
imagined throwing my leg over
and clutching you around your waist
and laughing like crazy and I didn't
In my dream as I finished your poem
I jumped on your motorcycle
and grabbed the waist of the girl
I only dreamed about at school
she was a couple of years older
and she never looked at me
but I looked at her and she was
in front of me on her motorcycle
as I held tight and we revved
down the streets in front of my
house and laughed and I shouted
I'm home I'm home

PART TWO: SHADOWED STARS

TO PAINT THE SHADOW OF CIRCUMFERENCE

surrounded by silence
call it wind
call it fog
call it light
we know a thing by the shadow it makes
on the flower that blooms in silence
when you are looking at the bird
which flies in the wind but disappears in low light
returning as fog covering the silence
of the shadowed Absolute

AT DUSK

going into the night
the air solidifies
into the heaviness of dreams
without witness, without the constancy
of other, without the dark side
of wonder, of the hidden what ifs
that magnify possibility, making the
dark night of life accessible in light
so bright you have to close your eyes.

SHADOWED STARS

hesitations we once took
for ordinary
change the tension of the night

Like stars at dusk
we and the egret
disappear to the world

emerge in night grass
remote as the obdurate heart
pulsing trochees of stress

gradual ambient sunlight
replaces the ambiguities
of our shadowed life

in the uncertainty of morning
we and the stars once again
wait for the silence of the dark

the egret fans its great wings
assumes its poised stature
becomes almost visible

UNDER THE SHADOWS OF THE NIGHT

always the silence
the unspoken words
that carry on the work of the day
the work of the solitary walker of the night
unburdened and unseen
by the heat of the sun

in the heavy time between
the world of dark
and the world of light
immovable in the yearnings of the heart
the stillness of the in-between
creates a space for touch
for the breath of the walker

the moon
rises and falls
lighting and darkening
this lonely street of the artist
beset by large lurking shapes
words erased by that shadowed bird
hiding like the stars at dawn
the untold life - unseen, unheard

no words
only the artist's mind
which knows no suns

to put out the silence

THE STORY GOES LIKE THIS

The gift-wrapped present
which had seemed
so perfect in the shop
which he had now carried for hours
down these confusing roads
and which was probably all wrong
and there she was in the window
      waiting for him
      waiting for the present
      that had seemed so perfect
he was hot now sweating in his new sweater
he had hoped would make him appear to be
      all the things he was not
he could almost see her just beyond the turn
      what would she think of his gift
      so perfect in the shop
but now like him and his sorry self
      clutching his sorry gift
if he could just keep walking
just walk up to the door
untrammeled by the pounding his heart
just those few more steps........

ON THE ORIGIN OF RITUAL

The Hughes Aircraft laboratory in California has developed a "tilt meter" so sensitive that it has been able to record lunar tides in a cup of tea.
    —Lyall Watson in *Supernature*

The moon turns. I pause, cup in hand.

The level drops and landlocked tide runs red.

As seaweed etches patterns in the sand,

the teacup tips to contemplate the dead.

I read the drying leaves the leaving left:

The ocean drained denies the moon its pull.

Fortune follows lines. The palm's bereft,

the tables turn and Tarot turns the Fool.

Years spin into hours, collapse in time.

The wafered moon, loosed from its earthly trance,

spirals, flashing holograms of rhyme

as poets match the dark side of the dance.

The ocean steeps in kettles brewing tea.

A drop of water comprehends the sea.

ARS POETICA: LIVING ON THE EDGE OF MYSTERY

for Warren Bellows

the title of your new painting

brings that small yellow

house into my ken

who lived here

who left this poem

on the edge of mystery

the wind shaping itself

into water tunneling past

faster than the supplicants

can stop it hoping for

a glass of pure water

wind-ward water quenching

the lives of those who held

still during the deluge

and held out their hands

soon filled with the promise

of love and

mystery

ARS POETICA: ON THE EDGE OF MYSTERY

Ah, a whole different experience
here, on the edge itself, the entire
room house trees that surround the artist's
intention and the fog, the fog rising in
fog wisps coalescing to give substance
to the air to the house to the water
that rushes past, to the boulders that
ground this visionary but substantial
image that expands creating its own
universe enveloping the minds that enter
into its mystery that is minds of all who
allow themselves to become the vision
they are perceiving here where it now has
found its place but of course it creates its
place as it rests first in the artist's vision
then in its collaborative expressions as the
force of its creation includes those who
witnessed its progression from canvas to
minds opening hearts to their own memories
of such houses such fogs such incipient rivers
such boulders such completion of exquisite
mystery

GENERATION
for Nora Fanshel

where it met the ground
suddenly surrounded by a fungus
that revealed the dying within

no obvious sign on this already ancient fir
just the marker for the experienced
eye to know the matter

how wise the dream to know
to preserve this heart section
its rings denoting the life long lived

which will with time
disintegrate with the aid of
the fungus, giving rise

to the young sapling
later to grow into another
magnificent douglas fir

AFTERTHOUGHT

The poem I didn't write
a sonnet stopped too soon
it never reached fourteen lines
never reached the moon
it lingers on the fringe
of the poem I chose to write
hidden stars at dawn
darkened by the night
words erased by that dark bird
my untold life   unseen, unheard

DIGGING TO CHINA

Chinese medicine
herbs, Confucius,
fonts of wisdom
so we thought
growing up

we dug a hole
and knew
if we kept going
we would end up
in an unfamiliar fairytale land

now whatever we pick up
in store or shop
we hear or see
made in China
and despair

but traveling there
we readjust
and recognize
the wisdom and the folly
of our own country

China, China, China

THE SHADOWS OF LOVE

on painting the shadows of love
through the way my houses reflect
who I am and what I value

Floors and walls: begin with floors.
first, spread out all the rugs in your house.
that is the first love, the basis of your life
they come from all over the world, the first
an antique shop in Alameda, then, an anonymous
woman who had outlived all her rugs,
followed by Turkey, straight from where it was made
and we watched the woman throwing the shuttle
over and over, and that rug, forty years later, is still strong
vibrant with its intricate design, like our love,
an ancient design, colors from nature.my

Then to the walls: In the poetry room, given to us by a beloved
student many years ago, before her death at twenty-seven,
a four-color lithograph of a woman who looks exactly like my
grandmother, even to her shawl, draped around her shoulders.
here, in our eleventh house, before we hung our first painting,
hanging above the buffet in all the houses where it has always
been, our first Warren Bellows painting, which he brought to our
house almost as an afterthought, to fill a space, now one of eleven
of his works, each one selected just because, once seen, we saw it
only in our home, and this is true of those brought home since I
have been the one carrying on alone. I always checked with her on
the last three.

There are other artifacts filing the house - sculptures from Alaska,
two Picasso ceramics, bronzes from artists of Afghan Hounds;
plates from everywhere, and of supreme importance to definition --
books. Books of every period of my life, from childhood; two,
gifts from my fourth-grade teacher, who introduced me to all my
future
passions --birds, Greeks myths, music, animals, trees.
there are books about alternate ways of knowing,

and they became the heart of poetry in my own life;
shelves of every aspect of my passion for teaching;
last but perhaps first, books by my friends, and other authors
I have known, and of course my own books of poems
and the people and lives that have inspired them.

Floors, walls, books, everyone will have his or her own definition
of love, but this is mine, for the time being.

TO LIVE IN EXILE

To live in exile—
To live an exile—
is to hold the memory
of the motherland in the heart.
Blood ties the exile to
a home remembered.
With time, the blood thins,
becomes water, becomes
the ocean between.

The separation complete,
the memory is just a faded photograph
in an album, You can almost
remember the faces.

Still, memory is jogged
by the smallest things: a line
of poetry; a gnarled redbud tree;
the touch of skin under hands that
smooth out tensions,
restore the balance
between two sides
of one world.

DREAM DATA

It is too late to begin the letter, the poem.
It is too late to push back the scrim of sleep,
to let the images through, to recognize
the parts of the dream and know the whole.

The parts, then:

"The way one mourns for a lost love or a dead child"
sounds aloud, a voice from the dream, a voice
reading a poem aloud, pushing the paper over
to the younger voice because a word is smudged
and I cannot read it. Recognizing, now, my voice,
reading the words of another, my own other,
my own words rendered through two voices,
two selves.

Always the two:
the girl, elusive, obsessive;
the woman, knowing again her other, younger self.
And as I know the mind of the other, I am the other
and resent the knowing and pull inward.

I close my eyes,
will my ears to shut out sound,
let my skin grow cold. I recognize
that I am unformed, yearning to be my older self,
and I let the woman draw me back to the sensate world.

For a time, I accept the eyes that read my mind,
the words that express my thoughts,
even before I have formulated them.
I find my solace in color and sound,
not in words or image, but in music and colors
beyond the spectrum until one day I find my dreams, too,
are shared, are open to a knowing I cannot tolerate,
and I break the bond that united me to my self.

Yet still, the girl, I dream,
and sometimes waken with words in my mouth,
but I will not say them. And I, the woman,
mourn for those lost poems
the way one mourns for a lost love
or a dead child.

SOUNDINGS

for Michael Franco, after reading his poem on silence

Oh, articulate silence, you loom large tonight
encompassing the secrets
so well hidden, you with your
clarity of vision, seeing beyond the
silence to the deep soundings
beneath the oceans as the whales
give forth song after song to our
unformed ears
what we hear are the melodious songs
of those great beings as they sing
the deep secrets known to our forebears
desecrations to our fractured world
prevent us from understanding
the depth and dark beauty of their songs
but in the echoes of their voices we sense
the truth and heartfelt sounds
that almost speak to us when we listen
to the mermaids in this ocean we call home

WOLF SPEAKS IN MYTH

I live in myth.
I am the stuff of ambiguity.
You will have met me years ago when I assumed the guise
of the grandmother, fooling that little red riding hood,
careless child, to be fooled by such a personification.
Sadly, you also met me when I protected that baby
whom her parents had left alone under my protection.
Recklessly they killed me when they arrived home,
seeing the blood, not noticing their beautiful infant
safe in her crib, not knowing the invading bear
had slashed me with his claws, leaving a trail of blood
while I protected the child.

Those early humans, having discovered fire,
sat in a circle around burning trees,
as I skirted the fire and the people.
Coming closer to the center, I stood at the edge
of their consciousness, waiting.
Above, the ravens circle, leading me to food,
and I shared that knowledge with people, and slowly
they saw that survival meant accepting my power,
accepting the intelligence that lurked
in the slant of my eyes.

Today, I am hunted, feared.
My domain has decreased with their numbers.
I look now to the people who remember,

who know that I am the one
who gave them their beloved dogs,
and I know someday the myth must reappear,
I wait for that time when raven and woman and I
will ultimately forge a new mythology.

UNTRANSLATED LANGUAGE

I write
I do not know
what I have written
I have written beyond these words
to their shadows
the hieroglyphs that hold
sacred meanings within
I cannot read these dark
marks that still live within
what has emerged
on this thin remnant of
etched stone
there is no translation
for the language
of the heart

THE PREDICAMENT OF BEING HUMAN

Fear and worry born of love
leave us easily distracted
by the overlay of memory -
the thin palimpsest
that almost reveals
the painting we depend on

it is raining lightly as we follow
the artist's stream between
the grey cliffs and ragged fence
always moving toward the pale
orange sunclouds just past
the final stand of trees

there miraculously the world bursts open
we trade the axis of rain and cold
for sun-heavy warmth that
never quite reaches the stone
pushing against the ribs -
the still beating heart

for Warren Bellows and his painting
"Beyond Walls and Boarders"

THREE: BEYOND DUSK

FRAGILITY

More and more frequently, I am reminded of the fragility of our lives, of our loves, of what we have built as our way of life. We expect it to go on forever, even as we know it will not. These are clichés, yet those of us who find our bedrock in language, say it again, over and over. We say it one way. We say it another. We might find we have written a poem about apple trees that bloom past their bearing, but it is the same thing we have said before. We might find, as I did in a sequence of coincidences, unlikely reconnections, one starting with a poem posted by a person on my favorite online list of writers. The poem began, "The ground before my doorway must be telling me something." I loved that line and immediately used it to begin a poem of my own. Of course, I then had to send my poem to the original writer, whom I did not know as he had not posted before to that group. We connected through Facebook and I then, checking out his list of friends, came upon the name and photo of a poet I had known very well some thirty-five years ago. She was a free spirit, constrained in a classroom. We exchanged poems and dreams, and she set off for Greece. All these years I have known that someday we would reconnect. And there she was, a friend of a poet I had just met online. She had gone to Greece, bought a castle remnant on the island of Kythera, wrote another book of poems, and came back to her family home in North Carolina. And now, free spirit still, she is setting off again for her Greek island home. How to explain these convergences in our lives? Just last week, another connection, the name of a friend from long ago, one with whom I shared a summer in the early days of the Bay Area Writing Project, 1974. We have seen each other occasionally over the years at a conference here or there. He lives and teaches in Louisiana. But now, on his birthday, his name comes up on my Facebook page. It has never been there before. We have not spoken or corresponded in many years. Surprised, I read the birthday messages from his many friends, but they are messages of sorrow. I write, to ask. He responds: his wife, his Sarah, whom he has loved for 43 years, is dying. Will die today, he writes, or tomorrow. It was a sudden, virulent cancer that settled in her spine. Such a gentle man. He says he can't stop crying. I cry for him, for his Sarah, for my friends, my partner, my self. For all of us. We have friends, we grow apart, we scatter across the country, across the world. We end up on mythical islands, the connections tenuous or buried under the everydayness of our lives. The years pass. We change. We gain weight. We lose weight. The seasons remind us of small things. The swallows come in May, leave in August. The dogs grow older before our eyes. I write into silence. Sometimes a miracle returns. The globe is round. It has no ends. We spin into space. We are dizzy with memory. We are ill. We recover. Some time it will not be so. But now we are well. We love each other. We love this life. It is a fragile gift.

MOVING INTO LANGUAGE

>we walk on the bones
>of our mother
>shape earth silence
>into elegy,
>mourn the lost words
>that lie with her,
>searching
>for our own lost song

It seems we were always talking,
my mother and I, and now, what am I to do with her stories,
her life, nowhere recorded
and I, who have somehow reached an advanced age,
have no one to leave them to.
there are fragments of her life in my poems,
but not all those outright memories,
the stories that she shared as we made the beds
together, or I stood on the dining room table
as she pinned up another dress for me,
perhaps talking about her sister, my aunt Prim, who made
patterns for dresses, how my mother once had to wear her
coat to school because her hand-me-down dress
was too small, or I watched the magic of
the homemade bread take shape from her
kneading and she talked about how her father
made an outdoor oven for baking bread for
their twelve children, I knowing I would get the heel

when it was still hot; we talked while doing the dishes together
before my little brother was old enough to help
and my older brothers were already out of the house,
and the magic of hearing her mother's voice calling
"Let's go make fudge!" at eleven o'clock at night
or Sunday mornings when my father came down for breakfast
and my mother made cornmeal pancakes with homemade syrup
while we learned from the paper how the War was going.
Am I to collect those pieces and weave them
into a collage of who she was, in addition to being
my mother, this small sampling of her whole self,
the woman I knew, whose stories only I know now,
braided into my own.

WOMAN MOVING OUT OF HER OWN MYTHOLOGY

This one is pale, webbed, ecru, like the curtains in the living room of our old house

It is faintly purpled, the edge of the rainbow dipping into yellow day

It is the color of dry earth as it crumbles when I prepare it for planting seeds

It stretches between two points, like the ends of a toy wooded ark

It bulges toward the left, a child's top squeezed out of shape

As I hold it, it just fills my palm, lengthwise, slightly folded

It feels solid, like a dry stone picked up in a riverbed, with bits of grass stuck to it

Along one side, a stretch of scar, dry and healed, pales the skin,

pricked as if nails had scratched it

distancing earth, it smells of the earth, but of dry earth,

faintly reminiscent of a cupboard long closed

it tastes of earth, like the one sweet potato that survived in my garden,

the taste fresh, textured, fibrous, barely sweet, astonishingly orange.

II

There is a long scar on her belly

my mother's scars were long and like the scars on the sweet potato,

healed stretching from navel to vagina

the birth of children made scars.

Their growth added weight to the scars

Like the skin on the potato, the scars are healed,

But the stuff of it is firm, solid, nourishing.
The skin is webbed, veiled. My mother's eyes
Were veiled, the skin thin, but the stuff of her was solid, firm.

She was earthy in her life underground she lived deep
In the earth, in touch with seasons, ripening unnoticed
by those who walked on the earth above.
She lived in darkness, believing it to be the only way to live.
not knowing the sun.
Yet she swelled and ripened on underground stems
And her children flowered in the sun, grew green
and did not know the source of their nourishment
came from the single sweet potato buried there.
The buried life, the buried life, we eat the buried life
and are nourished.

WILLIAM ERNEST CLAGGETT
my brother, 1934-2025

Reading your obituary
in the Havard magazine,
I am struck once again
with disbelief. It cannot be
true. Not you. Not my baby brother.
But the hard details are there,
among all the others, the same
year. Your classmates. The ones
you knew in those young days;
the litany of your life---your first
marriage, the two children, both
married, with lives of their own.
Then the second and perfect union
with your forever wife and your
new daughter, mother of your
beloved grandson. And your sister, me,
bonded to you since your birth when I,
five years your elder, claimed you
as my only baby brother.
And here you are, 90 years later.
All those important jobs done with
your gracious brilliance. All done
with the one word we saw over and
over in the condolences. Kind, they
remembered. Always done with kindness.
What you didn't know was, how like

your own father, who, also with kindness,
was able to create that space for those
thought to be unreachable.
Still, reading those words in the Harvad
magazine brings me up short and I wish
I could have one more day to tell you
how many lives you have touched, how
so many of us loved you, but especially me,
your only sister.

ADAGIO CANTABILE

Sometimes memory isn't really memory at all
it starts off that way, but underneath it is
the what if of your life

you write about the way you played
Beethoven when you were fifteen
but really you

are writing about what if you were still
playing Beethoven, the Pathetique's
the second movement

which cast such a spell over everyone
they closed their eyes and came
close to floating

leaving the old upright there
where it stood in the dining room
with you dazed and floating too

and everyone humming the familiar
melody of your childhood
translated into the

reality of your fifteen-year-old self
alone on the stage of every
recital you were ever in

and your mother and father
and brothers and aunts and even
Beethoven himself

smiling as you whisper
is this the way you hear it
now that you are deaf

and he nods and the tears
come and he sits down beside me
and puts his hands over mine

I TOOK HER NAME

I never thought to change my name.
Born knowing it was women I loved,
we did not have the custom reserved
for others. Marriage was not a possibility
even though we lived together,
worked together, shared everything—
dreams, clothes, dogs, bed.

After fifty-four years,
during which life changed
around us, laws that had seemed
written in stone, opened up
new ways of thinking about our lives.
We married, thinking it was for the cause
but found it was really for us.

Still, we never thought to change
our names. Until…
Until, not the way we planned it,
(we were to be together, somehow)
she was gone. I alone remained
living for both of us, and I wrote a poem,
signed it as usual, then, almost without
thinking, added the hyphen
and her name became mine…

A MEMORY

for Gishe Reyzl, on her 71st birthday

She was eleven.
Alone on the stage.
Not fearful; she knew the song.
She knew her grandparents were in the
multitude, the people
on the other side
of the lights.
She sang the song her grandmother
had taught her. She sang In Yiddish,
her grandmother's language
and the language she knew too.

She sang as she always did,
her voice sweet and true,
words from their homeland.
She sang directly into their eyes,
into their hearts.

When she stopped,
she waited
for the applause, for happy faces.
But no, they looked sad.
They were crying. They were all crying.
She almost began crying herself.
What had she done?

She didn't know what to do
with their tears.

ON TURNING 96, I ASK

Will I ever learn, I ask over and over.
Learn what you respond? As if there were an answer.

Learn who I am, learn who we are, learn what there is
to learn. What this life is we are born to live,

if not to learn what is. what is it that we love,
to drown in love is to learn to love, to fall, to fail,

to fall again and again. to fall in love, to love in falling
in love of another in love of one another, to fall

headlong we say into the moment of knowing
of being together to fall into the moment of knowing

we are ultimately alone, there is no other we fall
over and over in love, in terror, in aloneness

we ask will we ever learn who we are who we
might have been who we might yet become when

we know that we are the other and we are the beginning
and ending of our love and yet, there is the aloneness of

being the self and not the other or of being the self
and the other and we learn this over and over.

there was a tree and we learned to love the tree
and we knew there was no other

when I write will I ever learn, I know the answer is no,
I will never learn, because I am always the other
 yet still I ask will I ever learn.

TO TED KOOSER, IN LIEU OF A LETTER

There is a reason. There is a reason so many of us love Ted Kooser,

love the poems, love them for what they are and love them for where they take us. Love them for taking us to our own places. Places where we still live, no matter the geography, no matter the ages we have been and are, no matter that we speak in our own different voices--the ones we were given at birth, the ones we invented for ourselves growing up, the ones we have read over and over until we have become the poems we love, the Frost poems, the Emily poems, the Wallace Stevens poems, all our own now that we have felt them so often in our hearts. No matter the Ted Kooser poems that embrace our lives and loves and places we have lived over and over and never been to. No matter that we are 95 or 33 or twenty- one, just beginning.

And here I am, the day after. The day after the calendar said 95.

It is almost unnerving to be 95. On one hand, it seems perfectly normal, carrying on, writing, reading, dreaming, on the other, it seems a huge privilege; and in the middle, there are all the questions,…what else should I be doing? I think I am doing all I can do right now, especially since a new voice has entered my words. Felicity du Fleur has, I think, always been there, but quiet. Now she has spoken and desires to be given space and time. She is given to speaking in my old poetry voice, sometime as Petra who was trying to enter more often, but the heavy rocks kept her voice from being heard, and Felicity, as you see, was ecstatic to be a bigger part of my life. Felicity is freer than any of my previous voices, but she can be both light-hearted and serious, and, like Emily Dickinson, the serious always at a slant!

Back to my original thought in this piece... Ted Kooser. Thank you, Ted, for all your poems, which is to say, thank you for being who you are, sharing yourself with all of us who understand you. I personally think back to 2004 when you had just been named the Poet Laureate of the country, and I found you at the NCTE Convention, alone in a room set aside for teachers to stop in and talk with you. Well, lucky me, no one was there, and we had two hours to just talk! We came to our shared affection for the poems of William Stafford and the poem "Travelling through the Dark." "There is one line I don't understand," I told Ted. "I know which line it is." Ted responded, "and he doesn't understand it either." Then Ted told me that Stafford had talked with him about that line in a letter, and if he could find the letter, he would send it to me. Three months later, I received Stafford's letter in the mail. That is the kind of man Ted Kooser is.

That is the kind of person we all love and admire, and I, for one, hope I can be as honest and true as Ted Kooser.

THE CROOKED TREE, REVISITED
for JoAnn Smith

When I moved from Ohio to California,
to my new life, new love, I brought
a painting I had done, just one.
It was an oil, fairly large, and I was proud
of it. It was a tree, gnarled, misshapen,
but in my eyes beautiful.

My new love and I rented a cottage
high in the Berkeley Hills, and she brought
all the paintings she had acquired, perhaps
five or six altogether. We hung them, beginning
a pattern of filling our homes with art.

When we reached the end of what she had brought
she indicated that we were finished for the night.
My tree was still in its plastic wrap, unhung.
I didn't know how to suggest we might hang my tree.
"I can't, she said," It carries so much hurt, your hurt."

I was shocked, I hadn't thought of it that way. That tree
was me. Had I been so blind I didn't see that my tree
revealed how I really felt about my life before?

Perhaps that is why I balked at your poem, even though
I understood your metaphor, why your tree was precious to you
But kept seeing my painting, there on the bed, unhung.

And why, on my bedroom wall, there now hangs a
large, oil painting, misshapen but beautiful,
of a crooked tree.

AFTER WORDS

a cluster of birds
at the end
of the storm
fell into the breath
of the breeze
then flew into
the blossoming
fragrance
of after

NOT A SONNET FOR MARGARET ROONEY
on the occasion of her book launch

how to explain your journey to words
of memorable beauty - words that delve
into your life with utmost precision
clothed in metaphor that transcends today

attuned by your voice that makes magic of
heightened ecstasy - subdued sorrow -
readers who know your work
gasp with recognition

you asked for a sonnet and were I Keats
or Coleridge perhaps I could comply
but reaching for a comparison is futile
when confronted with perfection

your life encompasses many lives
one day - a psychologist, another
a farmer in your beloved Colorado
and within each place you have lived

you have carved out many lives:
lover, mother, elder sister, friend,
and in two groups dedicated
to poetry you are the poet supreme

luckily for us, your readers, many of your

incomparable poems are now
pouring down from this book -
the sky-opening *Wild Rain*

BEYOND THE CANVAS

The artist's brush traps
black eyes startled against
her vivid dream of
alizarin crimson buried
in the mass of huddled roots
the idea of a yellow garden
a distant memory
in this turned-back earth

walk through time on a map and
you are in another country
undefined with blurred
black edges

in her land of no boundaries
you never know where your world begins
you see a shield hammered into a chair
discover hidden eyes and faces
partially covered by black inks
keepers of time staring out
holding something back

EKPHRASTIC RENDERING

Given a choice
I opt for simplicity

Triangular shadow
extends meaning into space
the horse's head, profoundly at home
completes the purity
of the bowl

the disembodied loom large
and incoherent
heads small stretch to attached legs and arms
ending in forked
fingers and toes

It is with a sigh of relief
that I return to the minimal:
one color   one bowl.   the head of a horse

Only the blue backdrop
behind the mother and child
to give belief to the hint
of the artist's intent

LIKE NERUDA

grief does not just go away even though
some do not show evidence of it, which
does not mean it is not present
does not mean one did not love enough
does not mean this sudden sense of
abandonment has anything to do
with the length of loss
or its immediacy

it lies just beneath the edge of awakening
where one is subject to those moments
held so tightly that like Neruda we sing
the ancient rites of our soul-essence
briefly fulfilling our awareness
of being human

WORDS, ONCE WRITTEN
in Memory of Nancy Friedlander

With your death,
the line between states of being grows thinner and thinner.
"Who is living, who is dead", I write.
I have before me evidence of your living:
your poems, your stories, our talks.
Your quiet presence in my class.
Our lunches afterwards.
The death of your son, who became in the telling
a child in a story, a young man full of life,
unable to live, unable to die.
I have before me testimonies of a scaler of mountains,
a photograph, a poem, chronicles that earlier time
that never left your consciousness,
that found its way into mine, where I still see you
as I saw you that first poem, read aloud unwaveringly.
And I knew then that we would become friends.
Now I see you, after surviving
loss after loss - husband, son, brother - returning
to your country home, to your view of the lake,
to the birds at the feeders,
to your view of a life passed on to your daughters.

And for me, and for those of us who gather now to share
your words and our words written for you, there is no
lack of evidence that words, once written, continue
to bear witness to your life, a life well-lived.

THE SAME IMAGE, OVER AND OVER

She lies on the hospice bed
her dog draped over her
lying as still as she
bones giving shape to eternity
I sit by her bed like the dog
not moving in this amber light
the sun turning the arrangement
into a Vermeer painting
her face like ivory smooth as glass
a still life with a total absence of sound
only the steady beat of her heart.
Her words break the silence:
"There is so much to know,"
she says, my hand on her heart.

WHEN ONE OUTLIVES THE OTHER

Isolated and alone.
How many others can write those
words and know them to be true.
To the outside, I live in
harmony with friends in all directions.
That's the perception. But what is the
reality. Family gone except for visits several
times a year and the last brother gone.
Old friends gone many years ago.
In my house, surrounded by caregivers
thoughtful, considerate. For now, available,
but for millions, not. For me, life is
memory. Where I live. Outside
all is silence. My love gone ten years.
We never thought one would outlive the other.
No one would believe the loneliness.
New friends have spouses,
family, purpose. The essentials.
Days go by. A week. Still,
I know and cherish the other
in my silent internal world.

ON THE EDGE OF TIME

every poem I write I think
what if this is the last one?
every day I wake up and wonder
whether I will keep waking up
day after day forever and what if
this is
        the last crow
        the last poem
        the last dog
        the last hug
        the last great blue heron
        the last house
        the last love
        the last memory
        the last day

A TO MEMORY

I   The Birdwoman

No one else is alive
who remembers.
The future in the poem
is not beholden to its past.

Carefully I fill in the dates in April
only one birthday there
but March was busy with birthdays
and doctors

It is March and the poinsettia's red leaves
are still hanging, creating a future
that may outlast
the calendar.

Departures from the ordinary
the familiar, the prosaic, art
as technique, predictable as neurons
in the hippocampus

Move in the direction of tropes
undefined miracles, secrets, myths
Notice the visible quality of silence
drawing the line over the unsaid.

End with the image, don't explain.
The birdwoman
stands by the window
dreaming in cloud cover.

II   Saying the Unsaid
       for Madgik

Birdwoman returns

stands at the window waiting
      No, she hears, go to the door,
      open it.

    Far in the distance
    flash of movement
        then
            stillness,
                silence.
She turns
    sees in the
        window
what lives in the
    silence
        what was always
            there
beside her -
    his relentless
        devotion

MADGIK, MY SALUKI WITH RELENTLESS DEVOTION
August 3, 2009 - August 5, 2022

I knew when I first saw the photograph
of the dog that could be mine
he was already destined to be my dog.

He was five years old.
He had lived with an abusive woman all his life.
He had been beaten with a broom.

He had been rescued and returned to the breeder.
My partner had recently died, and with her,
our lovely saluki, Jason, who lay on her hospice bed.

I was doubly bereft. I called the breeder
who told me of a dog, a nephew of the one
who had followed my love as I knew he would.

She told me his history and wondered.
Was I up to the task. He had been deeply wounded.
Please, I said. Bring him to me.

He didn't want her to leave. kept going to the door,
expecting her to come back.
On the third day, he looked at me.

I heard him say, I will be your dog.
From that moment, he would not allow
anyone to come close to me.

He stood when I stood; he was always by my side.
He would lie down near me, but he never closed
his eyes as long as another person was in the room.

If I got up to go to another room, he was there.
It took eight months for him to allow another
person into his ken.

I had a poetry group meet weekly in my home.
Gradually, he established his ritual; he would greet
each person individually, then lie down where he

could keep his eyes on all twelve people. He gradually
learned to accept their pets, head down. one for each.
He never challenged those who were invited.

Eventually, he came to exert a powerful influence
of expectation on all of the poets. He became
the one who listened to each poem intensely.

One day, after his dinner, he came up to me
and said, clearly, I am going to be a happy dog.
No one is ever going to hurt me again.

And he was and no one ever did.
But he still slept with his eyes open
as long as another person was in the room.

JUST BEFORE DYING

       At dusk untrammeled
    by the bright light of consciousness
      by the egret motionless
          in the shadows
     by the trillium nodding in the stream
            coppery against the loose stones
     by the mockingbird mimicking morning
        from the high wires
by the soft padding of the quiet fox through
    the worn path below the vantage point
       of the morning crow
   spreading its wings
          silent in its waking
staggering incidents made only in one direction
     the mystery of precarity at a pivotal point of balance
       when no one is looking or seeing
   what is there
      all the time

UNTIL

Your story is not my story.
Your dog is not my dog.
You loved your dog.
He was the best dog in your world.
I loved my dog.
He was the best dog in my world.

We grew old.
I had to keep living.
He wouldn't know what to do without me.
I had to keep living so he would keep living.
That's how it was.

Suddenly he grew old faster.
As did I.

One day he just laid down and died.
As did I.

My dog is not your dog.
Still, your story is not my story.

Until it is.

CLARITY

the ground before my doorway must be telling me something
                                    —Dave Hopes

Not only the ground but the sky, the sky. Filled with swallows claiming the birdhouses one by one (what must it look like inside those wooden houses scattered around the edges of the orchard (are there eggs yet or perhaps baby birds?) but beyond the bird houses beyond the ancient apple trees jagged from the fallen branches deep in the grasses not yet mown providing cover for the deer oh the deer that leapt across the driveway on my way to get the mail and almost disappeared into the grasses but stopped, turned, and stared at me all the way down the road and when I walked back up to the house, there it was, still standing, still staring, and the dogs on the deck staring back, not barking, but beyond the grasses and the deer there is over the mountains a veritable   how to describe the color   a vibrant sunset that surrounds this house, this land, this bird space, this deer space, a sunset in the north, in the east, and south, too, and then I have to go into the house and climb up the spiral staircase to the only place where I can see all the way to the west, practically to the ocean, and yes, the sunset is there where it is supposed to be but not as bold not as purple not as red as in the east. I don't have any words for the colors that deepen and change as I look now for the deer but see only the birds beginning to settle into the approach of darkness and the sky, yes, the sky is telling me something. Everything startles in its transcendence…the ancient trees, contorted, hollow-trunked, stark against the new-meadow green, the white prints of the raccoon that traverse the newly painted fence top leading to the bird feeder, the seven crows strategically balanced on bare branches. Oh the clarity, if even for just this moment when we, like the crows, are still, waiting.

THE FOLLOWING IS AN ADDRESS GIVEN TO THE 50TH ASILOMAR ENGLISH TEACHER'S CONFERENCE IN SEPTEMBER 2000.

Words as Legacy, Silence as Gift: Reflections of a Teacher-Writer

Every year before the first class of the first day of school, I entered my classroom cocooned by silence. I felt the heaviness of promise, responsibility, hope. How was I ever going to establish the right tone. Somehow, I knew, instinctively, that it was all about tone, that first uncertain hour.

Then the bell rang, the students came in, their faces registering their own hesitancy, fear, hope, questioning...what kind of class would this be, what kind of teacher. A few familiar faces smiled and stopped by the podium to talk, and gradually, the class took shape.

I began by speaking the name of each person, asked for help in pronouncing some, knowing how important it is to get the names right, to focus even for a moment on each student separately.

And then, once again, it was the magic of September.

One of the things I love about being a teacher is that there is always another chance, another September, to get it right.

Eliot, in Burnt Norton (the Four Quartets), writes:

> *So here I am, in the middle way,*
> *trying to learn to use words, and every attempt*
> *is a wholly new start, and a different kind of failure*
> *because one has only learnt to get the better of words*
> *for the thing one no longer has to say, or the way in which*
> *one is no longer disposed to say it. And so each venture*
> *is a new beginning, a raid on the inarticulate....*
> *for us, there is only the trying.*

Each September (since 1961 for me), there is Asilomar. I never dreamed, that first year as I engaged in the conversation that marks our Asilomar tradition, I never dreamed that thirty-nine years later I would stand here and face all of you, from Leo Ruth, who chaired my first Asilomar group in a discussion of "The Picaresque Saint" to Walter Loban, whose presence still envelop me, to all the commission members who have been here, generally behind the scenes but creating every scene, every year.

I am aware, as I stand here, that I am standing in the shadows of those who have talked with us from this stage–Alex Haley, Anais Nin, Joseph Campbell, Robert Duncan, James Moffett–and some of our own–Miles Myers, Claire Pelton, to name just a few. To name these names is to take courage in the reality of the continuing conversation that is Asilomar. I would like to extend a special welcome to those of you who are here for the first time and hope that perhaps, thirty-nine years from now, one of you may be standing up here and think back to your first Asilomar.

I am here to continue the conversation, but, like the first day of school, how do I set the tone? "What are you going to talk about?" people kept asking. "Which conversation are you going to continue?" No one would be surprised if I said, "I am going to talk about standards–or about effective staff development, or authentic assessment of reading and writing. No one who knows me would be surprised if I said I was going to talk about poetry.

And they are right. I am going to talk about poetry.

The most important thing I know that we can give our students is the legacy of words–the image, the line, the stanza, the word. But foregrounding the legacy of words also entails that we are constantly aware of the background of silence.
In the far reaches of the background, I will be talking about reform–the standards, assessment, staff development, the high school exit exam–because there can be no effective reform without touching the poet in every person:

The legacy of the word is the ballast that enables us to take on these other challenges, not to retreat in the face of what are nearly overwhelming forces assailing us in education today. We can survive these forces if we remember who we are and why we are here. And why all our students need poetry:

Struggling readers can read poetry
Mathematicians lean toward poetry
Struggling writers can <u>write</u> poetry
Budding physicists <u>cannot deny</u> poetry
Environmentalists have to <u>save</u> poetry

Janice Mirikitani, San Francisco's new poet laureate, quotes Adrienne Rich in her essay *Breaking Silence*: "We must read/write as if our lives depended upon it." Janice goes on to say,

> And indeed our spirits are endangered if we see ourselves become numb from violence: race motivated hate crimes, anti-gay/lesbian/transgender/bi-sexual bashing, WAR. More children killing children, the glut of drugs in our poor communities, racial slurs by national candidates, and we are stunned at the lack of consequence. Does Language matter??
>
> If the power of the word penetrates deeply to our beliefs of who we are and the values that we hold dear, the world we wish to build for our children to inherit; and if that power can be written across the chalkboards of our schools, the pages of history and literature - the Web pages of the future - if poetry connects and humanizes us, restores our souls, THEN WE MUST READ AND WRITE (and vote) as if our lives depended on it.

This, from a budding physicist who could not deny poetry, who wrote because his life depended on it:

> Rough Draft
>
> *I wring this poem*
> *Like a wet rag, to bare*
> *Essential, but I can't ever*
> *Quite squeeze the rag*
> *Completely dry. Rough*
> *Drafts never smooth*
> *Perfectly, after all, just*

Even out to infinitesimal
Graininess, n-sided polygons
Disguised as circles.
Or (perhaps) they really
Metamorphose, as caterpillars
Will. If so, the final
Crisp wing conceals
Startling transfigurations.

Initial gropings, then:
The blind, deaf hand
Feeling the touch of water,
merely, and nothing less than,
The journey to poetry.
—Freeman Ng

And this, from a fifteen-year-old student who wrote this poem after being in this country scarcely a year.

Dedicated to the Alameda High School Teachers

Even though, my dearly loving teachers,
your time is as precious as all
the richest jewelry in the world,
it never would lose its valuable
signification of gold.

Always, you will fight a battle in
your country with a book in your hands
to defeat a war of ignorance
and will fill up with richness
knowledge of our Mother's Earth.

Afterwards, you are devoting your lives
without getting any medal of honor,
but in your consciences will remain
your lovely dedication to the students
with the placidity of tenderness.
—Mirna Lau

Freeman, an Advanced Placement student, and Mirna, a second-language student, (whom we now would label ELL), would not have connected in our school if it hadn't been for seeing each other's poems on the wall of a classroom that they shared at different times of the day. But they did connect, and they recognized the poetry of each other's words and worlds.

Students become different people when they see their poems on the wall, on web pages. Site after site of school web pages are now filled with student poems, an option I never even dreamed possible when I began teaching.

Those of us in the Writing Project have learned to say that we teach best what we know best, that we can write with our students and be better writing teachers. I always feel somewhat guilty when I talk about writing with other teacher-writers. I listen to friends as they share their methods of gathering up material for stories wherever they go, and I nod, agreeing that these are the ways of writers. But now I admit it: I *talk* about what they actually *do:* writing every day, keeping a journal, squirreling away the stories and voices of people in fast-foot restaurants. I don't even *go* into fast-food restaurants. And even though I *do* go to airports and coffeehouses and other places filled with stories, I rarely hold them in my head. I mean to. I sometimes think, "This is a scene Peter would turn into a great story!" – but I don't. On planes, I read mysteries; I seldom write.

What it comes down to is *I don't record my life*. When I say that, I am, in a sense, confessing to a missing element in my writerly nature. But that doesn't mean that I am apologizing. A missing element may be replaced by something different.

How is it then that I presume to stand up here and talk about myself as a teacher- writer? I want to try to explain my answer to that, to provide perhaps a different angle on what makes writing important–more than that–indispensable to all writers... and what makes writing poetry important for our students.

I'm not sure--this is an idea I'm just working out--but I think a have a clue as to how my approach differs, and I share it with you in case some of you may have been feeling uncomfortable, not "in your element" during workshops or classes in which you feel you must write along with your students, the freewriting, the journal-writes.

This is how it is with me: while my students record pages and pages of narratives about their lives, I fall into abstractions, into metaphor, into silence:

Why does it always come to poetry? Even in conversation, words move to line, stanza, demand a title. Leave out great chunks of thought. Glide over sentence parts. Leave space for silence. Expecting nothing back. And everything.

Etty Hillesum, who, in her diary *An Interrupted Life*, gives us the words of a brilliant, sensitive young woman living through the gradual Nazi encroachment of Amsterdam, moving first to Westerbork, the holding camp, and then boarding the train to Auschwitz, articulates the role of silence in writing.
Here are her words:

> Friday evening, 7:30. Looked at Japanese prints with Glassner this afternoon. That's how I want to write. With that much space round a few words. They should simply emphasize the silence. Just like that print with the sprig of blossom in the lower corner. A few delicate brush strokes--but with what attention to the smallest detail--and all around it space, not empty but inspired. The few great things that matter in life can be said in a few words. If I should ever write—but what?

I would like to brush in a few words against a wordless background. To describe the silence and the stillness and to inspire them. What matters is the right relationship between words and wordlessness, the wordlessness in which much more happens than in all the words one can string together. And the wordless background of each short story—or whatever it may be—must have a distinct hue and a discrete content, just like those Japanese prints. It is not some vague and incomprehensible silence, for silence too must have contours and form. All that words should do is to lend the silence form and contours. Each word is like a small milestone, a slight rise in the ground beside a flat, endless road across sweeping plains. It really is quite laughable: I can write whole chapters on how I would like to write, and it is quite possible that apart from these words of wisdom I shall never put pen to paper. But those Japanese prints suddenly showed me most graphically how I would really like to write. One day I would love to walk through Japanese landscapes. In fact, I am sure that one day I shall go to the East.

So, when I say that I don't record my life, I abstract it, what I mean is that I pay more attention to the silence than the sound–to the white space on a page than the black. That's not quite right. I pay attention to how the white space--the silence–affects the black—the sound. And of course, like Notan, the Japanese art form that involves a perfect balance between the fields of black and white, the other way around: a shifting field of black and white, of silence and sound

When I say I don't record my life, I abstract it, I mean that I transform the narrative of my life into metaphor. I frequently carry a line around a long time, without writing it down, until one day it just appears on paper with a kind of crystallized intent. The line I carried for years after my mother died was, "Who will tell her stories now?" And one day, at Asilomar, forced into language in my own poetry workshop, it found its voice as this small poem:

    Moving into Language

    We walk
    on the bones of our mother,
    shape earthsilence
    into elegy
    mourn the lost words that
    lie with her,
    searching
    for our own lost song.

The silence has given rise to the sound.

Wallace Stevens writes,

> *I do not know which to prefer*
> *The blackbird whistling*
> *Or just after.*

Which to explore, words as legacy, "the blackbird whistling" or silence as gift, the "just after." But what is the *whistling* without the *just after*? What are words without the spaces between? How can I deal with one without the other?

I will begin with words, with the sounds, knowing that the only way we can hear sounds is to create silences, the spaces between the sounds. First, my own legacy: to whom do I owe my love of language? How can I chronicle my own Odyssey, my attempt to get home to the Ithaca of my lifelong absorption with/in words?

Sound and silence. Word and space. The legacy of words:

The spoken word is my legacy, nothing written down. The stories began with my grandmother, lying in the double bed we shared on her long visits, listening to the stories of the child, her mother, who came from Wales to live with her American aunt and uncle, telling of the promises of school and a good life, but translated into the cold attic room, and washing dishes and laundry, and dusting and sweeping all of the rooms let out to boarders, and not going to school at all. And then, the best part, the gentleman boarder, twenty years her senior, who felt sorry for the fourteen-year-old girl and took her away and married her. There were those stories, over and over, told in the dark in her lilting Welsh voice.

And there were the stories of my mother's Scottish grandmother, born and raised on the small island of Tiree, mythic in my memory of the young couple on their wedding day, the groom going off on the ritual fishing expedition, the bride waiting on shore for the first catch of their married life. Then the storm, suddenly and fiercely catching the small fishing boat, sweeping the young man overboard to his drowning, the bride, watching from shore, seeing her life drown before her. If not for that storm, she never would have left the small island of Tiree, gone to Edinburgh, met my great-grandfather, borne my grandfather, moved to America, to Ohio, where he would marry the daughter of the young Welsh girl.

"Where did you get your interest in words?" I asked my mother, who loved to play Scrabble, work the crossword puzzle, and watch Wheel of Fortune. For it was words, not ways with words, but the words themselves that fascinated her. "I don't know," she answered." My grandmother learned Latin and Greek on Tiree. Your grandfather loved words; he knew most of Shakespeare by heart." I was staggered. Latin? Greek? Shakespeare by heart? My grandfather who had worked in the coal mines with his six sons all of his life?

And the five daughters, what of them? Words captured them, kept them in school, and made them into teachers, as well as world class anagram players. Aunt Carrie, the last time I saw her, a few months before her death at 89, beat me blind. Aunt Betty, the aunt whom I most resemble in intellectual and political interests, the aunt whose mind was always razor sharp, even when dulled by Alzheimer's, still responded to the wooden block letters, still made *worlds* out of *words*, the old familiar smile briefly flashing before the circuit closed over again.

Anagrams and Shakespeare. What is the connection? "Words, words, words." Words, through the grandfather from Scotland, son of the woman raised on the island of Tiree, where she, like the other children on that barren island, went to school, studied literature, learned it by heart.

In the small mining town in Ohio, one family read together in the evenings, by kerosene lamps; my mother, uncles, and aunts--all eleven of them--spoke "proper" English, often to the ridicule of the other children. Their speech has none of the southern Ohio linguistic patterns that would reveal their childhood home.
No one in the family had ever gone back to the island of Tiree. The name itself became Ithaca for me, carrying as it did the story of the

wedding day tragedy and representing the origin of my fascination with language. And so I wandered my way to Tiree for all of them--the aunts, the uncles, the grandmother, the mother--most of all the mother, to create the memories that they could not invent for themselves.

It was an Odyssey. There was water to cross. There was a small plane. There were rain and wind, cold summer weather in the Hebrides. And on the island, nothing taller than a shoulder-high bush that would not bend in the winter gales. Sheep and cows obscured homes built into the earth, roofs slanting up from the ground. The island seemed deserted as we walked to the tavern inn, the only accommodation; it wasn't until we opened the door that we discovered the center of the island, gathered noisily in the pub. From there we could see the graveyard where we found seven stones attesting to the sometime existence of the McDougals; and the next morning we walked to the school--the school where Flora McDougal had learned Latin and Greek, learned Shakespeare by heart, later to teach it to her son.

By these devious means, we receive the legacy of words, and I turn from words to silence, silence as gift:

How does silence inform the storyteller, the writer? "Everything comes out of silence," Alice Walker reminds us. "If you're silent for a long time, people just arrive in your mind."

In every life there are details of memory that are left in shadow. (How did she feel, Flora McDougal, when the boat did not return?) It is through these indistinct traces that a story gains its dynamic quality. (The grandmother, lying in bed with her nine-year-old granddaughter, telling the silences.) It is these traces, these gaps in our lives that compel the writer in us, that urge us toward completing our image of place, person, event; it is these silences that evoke the words that create our memories.

And I turn again to...the silences of the text. In every text there are details of setting, character or events that are left incomplete by the writer, that require the listener, the reader, to fill. It is these gaps in the text that bring the dynamic transactions of the listener, the reader into play. The ways in which the reader fills in these gaps become the "virtual reality of the work." And those of you who have struggled with designing a rubric to measure a student's proficiency as a reader know that the ability to fill the gaps is central to the act of reading.

Like the hologram, which exists only through the action of laser on object, and which takes a unique shape for each person "creating" this hologram, the poem, the story becomes a virtual reality only by the laser of the reader's perception on the "object," in this case, the composed text.

There are words that transcend our usual way of thinking about language.

Water. Rock. Fire.

These words are as central to our understanding as the metaphors that enable us to expand our knowledge. They are as deep as myth.

They are the archetypes that create of this ungainly world --one interpretive community. And so the concept of virtual poem takes on new meaning: it is not just the words, the writer, the reader; it is all these plus the symbolic archetypes that enable us to create at least parallel if not identical holograms.

"The poem makes meanings of the rock," Wallace Stevens says. In "The Poem That Took the place of a Mountain" he wrote:

It reminded him how he had needed
A place to go in his own direction,

How he had recomposed the pines,
Shifted the rocks and picked his way among clouds,

> *For the outlook that would be right,*
> *Where he would be complete in an unexplained*
> *completion:*
>
> *The exact rock where his inexactnesses*
> *Would discover, at last, the view toward which they had*
> *edged,*
>
> *Where he could lie and, gazing down at the sea,*
> *Recognize his unique and solitary home.*

The poem that I create from Wallace Stevens' poem will not be the poem he wrote or the poem that you read. Yet we will be able to talk about it as if it were the same poem because of the archetypal power of the word *rock*. In other poems, a less obvious connection may exist, but it will exist because of the symbolic nature of language. We may be unaware of the role of symbol in our work as we write, but living the conscious life allows us to discover new conjunctions of meaning as we read our own as well as others' work.

I am not suggesting that we plan our work by consciously "putting in" archetypal imagery. What I am suggesting is that we become conscious, aware readers of our own writing as well as of the writing of others. And, as mindful readers of our students' writing, we acknowledge their part in the linguistic community that we are constantly forging, over and over, with spiraling effects.

At this level, when we become cognizant of flickers of meaning that we had not consciously intended, we can begin the real work of writers: re-vision. The first step is easy–the inspired flow. But the next part is where conscious awareness becomes involved. For years I thought that I was purely a right-brain writer. I never revised my poems or papers.

Then, one day when Adrianne Marcus, working with my class as one of our poets-in-the-schools said to me, not my students, "Take out that last line. And start with line 5," I began to see how I could move from sometimes glib, unexamined poems to more considered pieces. I discovered, not without initial resistance, the act of re-visioning my own work. And as I came to this understanding, amazingly enough, so did my students! With Adrianne's help, I came to see–and to teach–that writing is an act of interpretation, no less than reading is an act of composing... and that we must be both composers and interpreters of our own work and of our students' work.

Writing from such awareness can help us learn to fix the elements of archetypes in our mind, reflect on how they can inform our work, and re-vision our poems. "The poem makes meanings of the rock." Even though our words may sound, to us, like Stevens' "scrawny cry," they, too, can carry us, and sometimes our readers, to "a new knowledge of reality." Both reading and writing, then, will be lifted to new heights (or drawn to deeper depths) as we give shape to the virtual poem.

The concerns we have for our students who are struggling to make meaning *from* the printed page, who struggle to make meaning *on* the blank page...we can address these concerns not by programmed, scripted lessons, but by giving them the legacy of words, by reading poems aloud, by having them find poems to read to us, by giving them strategies to fill in the gaps, by allowing them to find the connections between hand and eye and mind, and, yes, heart.

We can fill our rooms with books, our walls with words and drawings, *their* words and drawings, our hours with reading to each other the words that we have written, the words that others have written.

We can find poems in every language and ask students to read them to us. We can translate poems, short poems, and share our differing translations as we learn that translating engenders the closest kind of reading.

Poetry is not just for the Advanced Placement students, although in those classes, too, there is too often a dearth of time devoted to the writing and reading of it, but poetry is the primary kind of writing

that goes straight to the source of language for all the students.
who fill our classrooms each day.

We cannot afford to allow our classes to conform to a politically safe, reductive kind of curriculum that is bounded by state-imposed standards and examinations. If we provide access to the power and control of words, of poetry, our students will not only survive those examinations, they, like Faulkner, will endure.

Siobhan Campbell, an Irish poet who read recently at the Petaluma Poetry Walk records her son's emerging literacy in these lines:

> *Words draw meaning out of sound.*
> *That is what my son is teaching me.*

And later...

> *Soon he will learn "tree" then "leaf,"*
> *And say the world, word by word to itself.*

Word by word, and the silence between. It is difficult for an English teacher to be silent. *Try.* Read a poem aloud. Be silent. Wait for the first tentative voice to break the silence with the words, "I think...."
Moving out of silence, out of the white space—the distance between words, the distance between languages, the distance between us—Into that silence, a word spoken, in that silence, a word heard. How is it heard? How does your hearing change my utterance? How does my listening allow your words to enter the silence?

These words that are our legacy,
This silence that is our gift.

Fran Claggett-Holland

Fran Claggett-Holland, 2025

Fran Claggett-Holland is a teacher, poet, and dog-lover, who loves to see others' poetry dreams materialize. After many years of teaching at the high school and university levels, Fran taught poetry and memoir writing in the Osher Lifelong Learning Institute at Sonoma State University. She has given workshops across the country, as well as overseas through the Bay Area Writing Project. Fran's interest in brain research led her to develop approaches to reading, writing, and thinking using metaphorical graphics. She has received many awards, including the Lifetime Achievement Award from the California Association of Teachers of English. In Sonoma County, where she lives, Fran has received notable recognition from the Redwood Writers.

Fran has either written or co-written many books for teachers, including *Teaching Writing: Craft, Art, Genre; Drawing Your Own Conclusions: Graphic Strategies for Reading, Writing, and Thinking*, with Joan Brown; *A Measure of Success: From Assignment to Assessment in English Language Arts* (winner of the James N. Britton Award.) With Louann Reid and Ruth Vinz, she wrote the comprehensive *Daybooks of Critical Reading and Writing*. A collection of poems *Under the Wings of the Crow* was published by RiskPress Foundation in 2022.

THE PAGE POETS SERIES

Number 1
Between First & Second Sleep by Tamsin Spencer Smith

Number 2
The Michaux Notebook by Micah Ballard

Number 3
Sketch of the Artist by Patrick James Dunagan

Number 4
Different Darknesses by Jason Morris

Number 5
Suspension of Mirrors by Mary Julia Klimenko

Number 6
The Rise & Fall of Johnny Volume by Garrett Caples

Number 7
Used with Permission by Charlie Pendergast

Number 8
Deconfliction by Katharine Harer

Number 9
Unlikely Saviors by Stan Stone

Number 10
Beauty Will Be Convulsive by Matt Gonzalez

Number 11
Displacement Geology by Tamsin Spencer Smith

Number 12
The Public Sound by Marina Lazzara

Number 13
Record of Records by Rod Roland

Number 14
Strangers We Have Known by John Briscoe

Number 15
Cutting Teeth by Jesse Holwitz

Number 16
Other Scavengers by Lauren Caldwell

Number 17
Cueonia by Jesse Holwitz

Number 18
In the Museum of Hunting and Nature by Cynthia Randolph

Number 19
A New Species of Color by Tamsin Spencer Smith

Number 20
Busy Secret by Micah Ballard

Number 21
Out of the Blue by Fran Carbonaro

Number 22
Broadway Azaleas by Sunnylyn Thibodeaux

Number 23
War News II by Beau Beausoleil

Number 24
Hailstones by Justin Robinson

Number 25
Exile on Beach Street by Kevin Opstedal

Number 26
Everyday Villanelles by Kevin Arnold

Number 27
Uncollected Poems by Micah Ballard

Number 28
At Dusk by Fran Claggett-Holland

THE DIVERS COLLECTION

Number 1
Hôtel des Étrangers, poems by Joachim Sartorius translated from German by Scott J. Thompson

Number 2
Making Art, a memoir by Mary Julia Klimenko

Number 3
XISLE, a novel by Tamsin Spencer Smith

Number 4
Famous Dogs of the Civil War, a novel by Ben Dunlap

Number 5
Now Let's See What You're Gonna Do, poetry by Katarina Gogou translated from Greek to English by A.S. with an introduction by Jack Hirschman

Number 6
Sunshine Bell / The Autobiography of a Genius, an annotated edition by Ben Dunlap

Number 7
The Profound M: found photos paired with poems by Tamsin Spencer Smith with an introduction by Matt Gonzalez

Number 8
The Glint in a Fox's Eye & Other Revelations, volume one of a three-part memoir by Ben Dunlap

Number 9
The Origins of Bliss, volume two of a three-part memoir by Ben Dunlap

Number 10
Proud, Open-Eyed and Laughing, volume three of a three-part memoir by Ben Dunlap

Number 11
Esmerelda's Story, a historical novella by Mary Julia Klimenko

Number 12
Private Instigator, a Journey through the Underworld of Disorganized Crime by Steve Vender

Number 13
Dreaming as One, Poetry, Poets and Community in Bolinas, California 1967-1980 by Kevin Opstedal

Number 14
Art Writings: 2008-2024 by Matt Gonzalez

Number 15
Joey Chestnut's America: Politics, Patriotism and the Future of Democracy by William W. Sokoloff

www.ingramcontent.com/pod-product-compliance
Lightning Source LLC
Chambersburg PA
CBHW051656040426
42446CB00009B/1157